Designed and produced by
Albany Books
36 Park Street London W1Y 4DE

First published 1979

Published by Chartwell Books Inc.
A Division of Book Sales Inc.
110 Enterprise Avenue
Secaucus, New Jersey 07094

Design: Jerry Wells
Picture research: Mary Corcoran

Acknowledgments

I am indebted to the following people
and organisations for their co-operation
and help: The Guide Dogs for the Blind
Association; Mr Peter Heap, Senior
Press Officer of the National Coal
Board; the Metropolitan Police,
London; the Commanding Officer of
the RAF Police School, Newton,
Nottinghamshire; HM Customs and
Excise; Mrs Barbara Jackson of
Beauport Park Riding Stables, St
Leonards-on-Sea. Thanks are also due
to Messrs Allen and Unwin for
permission to quote from Josiah C
Wedgwood's *Essays and Adventures of a
Labour MP,* London, 1924.

Working Animals

Jean Cooke

 CHARTWELL BOOKS INC.

Contents

Bel. BB. 12-5-79

Pages 4 & 5: *A Mongolian herdsman on horseback working with a lasso on the end of a long pole.* (ZEFA, J Bitsch)

Left: *Teatime for the trainer. Flash, a Californian sealion, brings a cup of tea to the girl who looks after it.* (Heather Angel)

Introduction

Ever since the first wild dog crept cringing into the firelight outside the cave of Stone Age Man, seeking warmth and food, people and animals have been in partnership. It has been a one-sided partnership, for Man has always dominated the animals he has taken into alliance. Yet in return the animals have usually enjoyed Man's protection, and many kinds owe their very existence to controlled breeding.

Humans have used animals in two ways. Some animals are kept to 'do their own thing' and thereby supply us with food and clothing. Cattle, sheep, goats, pigs, poultry and silkworms are among these. However even such unlikely creatures as spiders have been put to use by Man. When bombardment from the air first became possible, no wire could be drawn fine enough to fashion the graticule (crossed lines) in bombsight eyepieces, and a spider's web behind glass provided an accuracy Man could not reproduce. Members of the second class of animals serve Man through their work. True, much of that work relies on their natural instincts and abilities, but

in almost every case each animal has to undergo training for its duties and display a degree of skill and intelligence in carrying out the tasks allotted to it. It is this second group of animals which forms the subject of this book.

Before the Industrial Revolution of the 18th and 19th centuries people depended on animals for a large part of the power they used. The wind supplied them with force to grind corn and drive ships across the oceans, and the power of running water turned mills and, later, worked the hammers of iron forges; but for land transport, tilling the soil, pumping water and any other tasks requiring power, people were dependent on their own muscles and those of the animals they tamed. Those animals could justifiably be granted a large share of the credit for the development of civilisation in the world. It is very noticeable that the most primitive societies which have survived into modern times, such as those of the Aborigines of Australia and the Stone Age tribes of central New Guinea, have made little use of animals in developing

Pages 8 & 9: For centuries people relied on animal power to drive pumps and other machines; this bullock-driven well is still in use near Lucknow, India. (Spectrum)

Right: The Dingo of Australia is a semi-wild descendant of dogs kept by the Aboriginal settlers of the land. (ZEFA, D Baglin)

Below: Another example of animal power still in use: a donkey-powered thresher in Majorca. (Spectrum)

12

their way of life. The dog was the only domesticated animal of the Aborigines, and this animal, surviving today as the wild dingo, was taken into the continent by Aboriginal settlers in prehistoric times. Few of the marsupial animals which are native to Australia lend themselves to domestication.

The taming of animals came comparatively late on in our history. Modern Man *(Homo sapiens sapiens)* developed something over 35,000 years ago, while primitive Man *(Homo sapiens)* had existed for more than 300,000 years before that. Cattle and sheep were domesticated something over 9000 years ago, and the alliance between Man and dog probably came before

that. The horse was tamed by at least 3000 BC; we know this because a clay tablet of that date containing an inventory of horses has been found in the ruins of the ancient Persian city of Susa. By 2000 BC most civilised peoples possessed tamed horses, and used them for riding.

The first and longest chapter in this book considers those animals which help us with our work. Next comes the use of animals in sport, involving just as much work but for different ends, followed by animals as entertainers, and as guides and protectors. Finally there is a brief account of the ways in which animals contribute to research, particularly in the field of medicine.

Right: *A mule carrying slag to a coal tip at a mine in Spain.* (Robert Estall)

Below: *The so-called 'Standard of Ur', a Sumerian mosaic tablet made around 2900 BC showing a war chariot drawn by two asses — early evidence of the use of animals for work.* (Michael Holford Library)

Hard at Work

14

Of all working animals, the horse has probably had the biggest part to play. As we have seen, horses were domesticated about 5000 years ago. At first they were probably used for food, but in time their value as transport became apparent, though there is no way of telling where or when men first learned to ride and to break horses for riding. Probably this event, so momentous for the future history of both man and horse, took place in western Asia, where most of the early civilisations of the world developed.

In prehistoric times the horse's ancestors roamed every part of the world except the frozen wastes of Antarctica, and Australia, the island continent which developed its own group of mammals, the marsupials, while the rest of the world went on to the more highly-developed placental mammals (those which give birth to fully-formed babies). In the Americas the horse died out, though how and when is still not known. The modern horse appears to have developed about a million years ago, probably in central Asia. From there it spread east to China, and west to Europe, south-western Asia and Africa. Few wild horses still survive. Of the true horses, the only wild ones surviving are Przewalski's horse, of which perhaps a couple of dozen still roam the steppes of Mongolia, and the zebras of Africa. The tarpan, the wild horse of Europe, died out in 1851 but has been bred back from surviving stock with some tarpan blood, and a small herd now roams the Bialowieza Forest on the frontier of Poland and the Soviet Union. The wild white horses of the Camargue in southern France are descendants of domesticated horses brought into the region with the hordes of Attila the Hun.

Top right: *Przewalski's horse, which roams the Mongolian steppes. Apart from zebras, these animals are the only true wild horses left.* (Natural Science Photos)

Right: *The white horses of the Camargue in southern France roam free, but they are only semi-wild, and many of them are captured and broken for work. The foals have black coats, which turn white as adulthood approaches.* (Hans Reinhard)

The horse in its early years of domestication was only a riding animal. For a very long time it was indeed the main animal for this kind of work, since archaeological evidence, what there is of it, suggests that both camels and donkeys were ridden at a much later stage. From the very first the horse appears to have been guided with a bit and bridle, and by the 300s BC most of the basic kinds of bits had been invented. By that time, too, stirrups came into use, and saddles followed about 500 years later.

Horses were not the first animals to draw ploughs or pull carts: oxen were used for this purpose, and the form of harness that was devised for them was the yoke, a wooden bar linking two animals side by side. The oxen were attached to the yoke by straps. This kind of harness did not suit the anatomy of a horse, because one of the straps passed across the front of the animal's neck, interfering with its breathing and so limiting the amount of power it could develop. Sometime around AD 500 the

Below: *Ploughing with oxen in Portugal. Note the simple yoke linking the two beasts.* (N.H.P.A.)

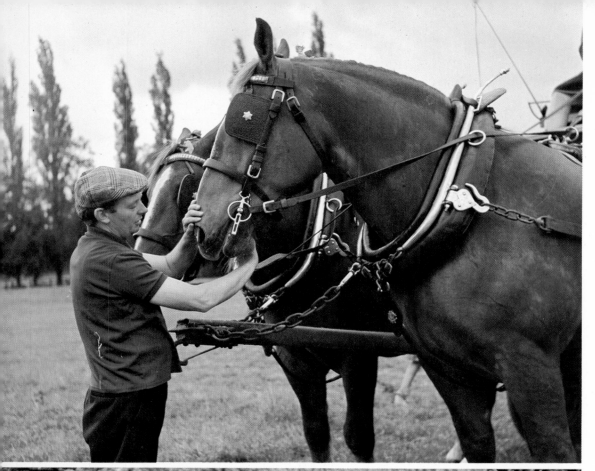

Top left: *These Suffolk Punches show very clearly the different harness used for horses — the horse collar, which enables a horse to exert maximum power when drawing a load.* (Spectrum)

Left: *Examples of horse tack: in front of an ordinary riding saddle are several kinds of bits: left to right, a Kimblewick (ideal for strong ponies); a Scamperdale, a kind of Pelham bit used for powerful horses; an ordinary snaffle bit; a Mullen-mouthed Pelham; a German egg butt snaffle.* (Spectrum)

Chinese invented the modern horse collar, which sits on the horse's shoulders in a way that enables it to pull as hard as it likes without upsetting its breathing. The horse collar was introduced into Europe about 300 years later. It reached its present form in the late 1200s, when it produced a revolution in animal power which has been compared with the revolution in the steam-engine that James Watt triggered off when he invented the condenser. With a modern horse collar a horse can produce more than four times the power it could with the older kind of harness. In particular, this enabled farmers to plough their land more efficiently.

Different breeds of horses are needed for riding and for other kinds of work. Saddle horses are comparatively light in build, often fast, and have lively temperaments. Many of them are thoroughbreds, horses of Arabian stock bred originally for racing (see pages 53-63). Thoroughbreds have been crossed with other types of horses to produce various kinds of riding horses. For example, the Irish hunter is a cross between thoroughbred and Irish draught horse stock; the American

Below: *A bloodstock or thoroughbred horse and youngster. Thoroughbreds are ideal for racing, eventing, polo and competitive riding.* (Spectrum)

18

A pure-bred Arab. Arabs are good for long-distance work, but are more contrary by nature than thoroughbreds. (ZEFA, W L Hamilton)

quarter horse, much favoured by cowboys, is a thoroughbred crossed with Spanish horses; the French trotting horse is a mixture of thoroughbred and Normandy stock. Thoroughbreds are all descended from just three Arabian stallions; in the same way one of the most famous American breeds, the Morgan horse, is descended from one stallion — believed to have thoroughbred blood in him — which was given to a Vermont schoolteacher, Justin Morgan, in the early 1790s in payment for a debt. The stallion, which became known as 'Justin Morgan's horse', proved to be exceptionally versatile, and equally useful as a plough horse, racehorse, or harness horse for trotting races. What was more to the point, he passed on his qualities to his offspring. He was eventually bought by the US Army, to spend the remainder of his 29-year life at stud. Present-day Morgans are bred for riding, and another breed, the Tennessee walking horse, is descended from the Morgan horse with some thoroughbred ancestry as well. The Tennessee walking horse has a quiet temperament and a brisk, comfortable pace.

Top right: A Welsh stallion; this breed is popular as a child's riding pony. (Spectrum)

Right: A Tennessee Walking horse pacing — that is, moving both legs on the same side of its body together. The raised tail is produced by docking. (Sally Anne Thompson)

Far right: The Quarter horse, a powerful animal, is a favourite with cowboys and other Western riders because of its speed and agility. (Sally Anne Thompson)

Right: *A Morgan horse mare and foal: the Morgan is one of the most popular general-purpose horses in the United States.* (Sally Anne Thompson)

The heavy horses, which are seldom used for riding, are among the toughest workers of the animal world. Among the biggest, and perhaps the most famous, is the English Shire horse, descended from the Great Horse of the Middle Ages. Shire horses have long been used for the very heaviest kind of work on the farm and pulling loads. Very similar to the Shire is the Clydesdale, which has Flemish horse in its ancestry. The third kind of English heavy horse is the Suffolk Punch, bred since about 1500. It is invariably of one colour — chestnut — though of several shades. All present-day Suffolks are descended from one notable stallion, foaled in 1768, and known as 'Crisp's horse of Offord', Thomas Crisp of Offord being his breeder. Almost as popular in England is the great French work-horse, the Percheron. This reliable draught horse was imported into England at the time of World War I, and in the 1880s thousands were imported into the United States. For a heavy horse it is remarkably active, and it is more compact than the largest of the Breton horses, which are also popular as work horses in France. Other notable heavy horses include the Dutch draught horse, which is widely exported, and the Brabant of Belgium, sometimes called the Belgian horse.

For drawing coaches, one of the principal means of travel before the development of the railways in the 1820s and 1830s, a horse midway between the light riding horse and the heavy cart or plough horse was needed. The Hackney, bred in England and used in the United States, was one of the most popular. Friesians, from the Netherlands, are also much used.

Horses have many advantages for local delivery work, and a small number are still used in many parts of the world. Several British breweries keep teams of horses for use in London, and for loan

Below: *A pair of English Shire Horses ploughing. These gentle, mighty animals are popular as working horses the world over.* (Bio-Arts, David M Burn)

Top right: *A Percheron mare. This French heavy horse closely rivals the Shire as an agricultural draught animal.* (Spectrum)

Right: *Horses are still used for delivery work in cities by some firms — in England, notably breweries. Here two Shires draw a wagon laden with barrels of beer.* (Spectrum)

for important ceremonial occasions. Roundsmen delivering bread or milk, and making regular calls at scattered houses in a road, would find that their horses knew the round as well as they did, and would move from one stopping place to another without being told.

Those of us accustomed to the busy city streets of today, full of the roar of motor-car and truck engines and heavy with the fumes of their exhausts, can have little idea of cities only 70 years ago, when automobiles were in their infancy and horses still provided the bulk of the traffic. Most vehicles still ran on iron-tyred wheels over stone sets, producing a roar little if any less than today's internal combustion engines, while the smell of horses and their droppings was everywhere. Those were the days when it was customary to put down straw in the street outside a house where someone was gravely ill, just to dampen the noise of wheels and hooves. Traffic jams were common, although the pace of travel was slower — how much slower is shown by the fact that my father-in-law, going to school in the 1890s, used to race — and beat — the horse buses of his day, thereby saving the penny fare. Fire-engines were also horse-drawn, and an impressive sight they were, sparks flashing under the flying hooves of the splendid horses that were used, and the bell clanging its warning.

The first trams were also horse-drawn, and they provided a link with two other forms of transport, the canals and the railways. Although manpower (and womanpower too) was used to pull barges along the canals, wherever suitable tow-paths were available horses were used instead. The canals were an amazingly economical way of moving heavy loads, albeit slowly. One horse could pull two laden narrow-boats — about 21 metres (70 feet) long and just over 2 metres (7 feet) wide. In Britain and the United States high-speed canal boats for passengers were developed in the early years of the 19th century, reaching speeds of up to 13 kph (8 mph) — five times as fast as many of the freight boats.

Opposite top right: *Horse trams were a familiar sight in many city streets before the introduction of electric power. This surviving example is used for holiday traffic in Douglas, Isle of Man.* (Spectrum)

Bottom right: *A mule carrying slag to a coal tip at a mine in Spain.* (Robert Estall)

Below: *This print of 1881 shows a horse-bus rolling through the slush and ice of a Paris street in winter.* (Mary Evans Picture Library)

Tramways, using first wooden rails and then iron ones, linked the canal docks with industrial production centres, such as coal mines. Horses, mules and donkeys drew trains of wagons along these tramways. The tramways had a much earlier origin, since they were used in English mines as long ago as the 1500s. The motive power was often provided by women in those days. By the 1700s horse-drawn railways were being used above ground at the mines. The earliest American railways were all horse-drawn, but as soon as the first successful steam-powered railways came into operation in the late 1820s the days of the railway horse were numbered. In 1830 a US locomotive builder, Peter Cooper, was challenged to prove his engine, the *Tom Thumb,* against a stage-coach horse in a race along parallel tracks of the Baltimore and Ohio Railroad. The horse won — but only because of a mechanical mishap in the locomotive.

The use of horses in coal mines has not completely stopped, and a handful remain in use. In Britain the numbers of so-called pit-ponies have fallen from more than 20,000 in 1946 to 139 in 1978. The remaining pit-ponies are confined to a few mines in north-east England and south Wales, where there are difficult geological conditions. The pit-ponies are used to move supplies up into new headings before mechanical haulage can be installed. They are not used for coal haulage. The use of horses is reviewed every six months, and it is hoped to phase them out completely before long.

Only geldings are used in the pits, and they must possess a steady and equable temperament. Peter Heap, senior press officer for the National Coal Board, who once drove pit ponies himself, says: 'A strong rapport builds up very quickly when a horse and driver spend several hours together every day. Few drivers fail to bring an apple or some other favourite tit-bit for their animals, and a horse soon learns to distinguish his own driver's footstep and will respond to gentle instructions far better than to shouted orders.

A Pit-Pony working underground. It is not hauling coal, but moving supplies to a new coal face before machines can be installed. (National Coal Board).

'Stories of horses warning men of impending danger are not all apocryphal: I have seen a horse gently nudge his driver away from an area of unsound roof, and in the days when portable lights were less reliable than today, many a horse led his driver back through the darkness of roadways after his lamp was extinguished.'

One other group of animals works in the pits: birds. They are used to test for the presence of the deadly carbon monoxide gas after a fire or explosion in a mine. So far nobody has been able to make an instrument which can detect the presence of carbon monoxide so quickly and reliably as a small bird. Canaries are generally used. When there is an emergency, rescue teams take a pair of birds down the pit with them in a cage. As they proceed underground the men watch the birds carefully. The signs of carbon monoxide poisoning show when the birds start fluttering their wings and sitting at the bottom of the cage instead of on their perch. As soon as these signs are seen the team withdraws to a part where the air is fresher. The team has breathing gear with it, and if a bird becomes unconscious it is revived with a whiff of oxygen.

Top: *Donkeys are used in many countries to carry incredibly large loads, like these in Spain.* (S C Bisserot)

Left: *This canary is being watched carefully for signs of being affected by carbon monoxide in a mine. As soon as it flutters to the bottom of its cage the rescue men withdraw to fresh air. If necessary the canary is revived with oxygen.* (National Coal Board)

People tend to think of horses in connexion with agriculture, but they were not extensively used on European farms until the 1300s. Up to that time the main beast of burden on the farms was the ox, as shown by such medieval terms as the oxgang, which represented one-eighth of a 13-acre (5.26 hectare) ploughland. Oxen were (and in many places still are) used in large teams, four or eight being common. Oxen were still used for ploughing in England — one of the most highly developed countries in its farming methods — as late as 1926, and in many parts of continental Europe they are still so used. In tropical

Top: *American Indians quickly took to horses when the Europeans introduced them to the continent. This horse is pulling a travois, the traditional Amerindian wheel-less 'wagon'.* (Jas. J Hill Ref. Lib.)

Left: *Oxen are used in many parts of the world; this hay-wagon was photographed in Romania.* (Bio-Arts, David M Burn)

countries cattle are the normal animals used for ploughing, especially in Asia and America; they are rarely used in Africa for such work. Buffalo, which are close relatives of the domestic cattle familiar in Europe and North America, are often used as work animals in Asia.

Another Asian beast of burden is the yak, a large, shaggy-haired member of the ox family which lives in Tibet. The animal's thick coat which has hair falling almost to the ground makes it able to resist the extreme cold in its native habitat, which is between 4300 and 6100 metres (14,000-20,000 feet) above sea-level. More than most animals, the yak is an all-purpose servant of Man. It provides milk, meat and leather, its long hair is spun into ropes, and its dung is often the only available fuel. However, in addition to this passive role, the yak is used extensively for carrying loads, and it is also used for riding. It would be fair to say that civilisation in Tibet is largely dependent on the yak.

Another example of an animal with specialised value in a particular environment is the camel, now known only as a domesticated animal. There are some wild herds, but they are descended from domesticated animals which escaped long ago. Camels are particularly suited to life in the desert. They can feed on vegetation that few other animals could live on, such as dried grasses, thorny twigs and other coarse food — just what is available in desert regions. The camels' humps are storehouses for fat, which they build up when food is plentiful, and can draw on when the diet is poor. Moreover, a camel can break down some of that fat store to provide water, so it can go for long periods without drinking — more than two weeks. A thirsty camel may drink as

Right: *In addition to their traditional role as 'ships of the desert', camels are popular in the tourist trade. These camels in the Canary Islands are carrying pairs of riders, in special double seats.* (S C Bisserot)

Below: *The yak of the Himalayas is an all-purpose beast of burden and riding animal. This Nepalese yak is carrying two sacks on a pack-saddle.* (Spectrum)

much as 115 litres (25 gallons) of water at a go, replacing in a few minutes the water loss of days.

In addition to its ability to survive on minimum food and drink, the camel has other physical qualities which fit it for life in the desert: soft, broad feet for walking on sand; long eyelashes to protect the eyes from blowing sand; and the ability to close the nostrils to keep out particles. Its long legs enable it to cover considerable distances at speed. There are two basic kinds of camels: the Arabian, which has one hump, and the Bactrian, which has two. The Bactrian camel can travel longer distances at a time than the Arabian, though at a slower pace: for example, a day's journey of about 50 kilometres (30 miles) carrying a load of 180 kilogrammes (400 pounds) is not uncommon. There are two kinds of Arabian camels: one is bred for load carrying, the other, often called the dromedary, is a swift-paced riding animal. For centuries camels have been used for transportation in the desert

lands of south-western Asia and northern Africa, and despite the development of desert-proof motor vehicles their day is far from over. They are also used in parts of the Indian sub-continent. Camels have been imported into Australia and North America, and a few have run wild; no North American feral camels are now known, however.

The camel's close relative, the llama, is an important pack animal in the Andes mountains of South America. Like the camel, the llama can go for long periods without drinking, and it feeds on poor vegetation, such as is found in the highlands where it roams. Llamas are sure-footed animals, which can pick their way safely over mountain trails. They have the same stubbornness as the camel, and will spit at people or other animals that annoy them. For hundreds of years the llama has been an important asset of the South American Indians. Like the yak, the llama is an all-purpose animal, providing food, wool and leather as well as transport.

Top left: *The traditional use of the camel: a Tuareg tribesman of the Aïr Mountains of north-western Niger.* (Spectrum)

Below left: *Farmers with only a few animals often have to yoke two very different beasts together for some jobs: this Moroccan is ploughing with a camel and a donkey.* (Spectrum)

Below centre: *Mules are all-purpose animals: this one is pulling trolleys along a tramway at a Greek salt-works.* (Spectrum)

Below: *In India the bullock is used for all sorts of work — even mowing the lawn!* (Spectrum)

The largest of all land animals is the elephant, and it is also one of the most skilful workers. There are two kinds of elephants, African and Asian. The African elephants are larger, but less easy to train. Nearly all the working elephants of the world are Asian elephants. A bull Asian elephant can be as much as 2.7 metres (9 feet) tall, and weigh up to 5400 kilogrammes (5 tons 800 pounds). With its pillar-like legs, huge curving tusks and long, flexible trunk an elephant looks a very clumsy animal, but this is far from true. It can move silently through the jungle when it wishes, and tiptoe through obstacles with little trouble. Its most remarkable feature is its trunk, a nose which has become elongated to nearly 2 metres (6 feet) of powerful muscle. The elephant has a very keen sense of smell, but it can use its trunk for many other purposes. It can draw about 6 litres (10½ pints) of water into its trunk, which it can then squirt into its mouth for drinking, or over its back for a cooling shower. The sensitive tip of the trunk is prehensile, and can be used for picking up small objects and for other delicate operations, such as untying ropes or sliding back the bolt of a door. This same trunk can send a man flying or lift a heavy baulk of timber. The tusks are also useful for work: they can help to support a log, or lever an object, or dig; but even a tuskless elephant can do much useful work. Elephants can carry very heavy burdens over tracks where no vehicle could go, and they can drag unwieldy loads along the ground.

Elephants are long-lived animals, and their training takes proportionately long. It lasts from about the age of eight years to twenty, during which time they contribute little in the way of work. An elephant's working life is about another thirty-five years. In the teak forests of Burma and other parts of Asia elephants are invaluable because they can go where no machine can, and indeed their work is necessary for constructing tracks and building bridges so that trucks can be used. Elephants think as they work, as people who have watched them piling logs will attest: they coax the logs into position, and their understanding of the orders that are given them is almost uncanny. Confronted with a new situation, an elephant will improvise, thinking out what to do and not just following routine. Not that elephants are averse to routine: at one Burmese sawmill the elephants understood the hooter for the midday break just as well as the men, and downed tools the moment it sounded.

Top right: *A team of dogs sets off with a sled.* (N.H.P.A., James Tallon)

Bottom right: *Large dogs are used as draught animals in several countries of western Europe; this St. Bernard is delivering the milk.* (N.H.P.A., Brian Hawkes)

Below left: *An elephant using tusks and trunk together to lift a log.* (N.H.P.A.)

An elephant going to work, carrying her lunch. (N.H.P.A., Douglas Dickens)

Dogs are particularly useful for their work in tracking and guarding, as will be seen later, but some breeds have value as workers in other ways. Of all the dogs used for transport, the most famous are the Huskies of the Arctic. These dogs have enormous stamina and can stand up to cold well. The Eskimos of the frozen north use them as sled dogs, and they have been invaluable for polar exploration. A team of 7 to 10 dogs harnessed to a sled can haul a 450 kilogramme (1000 pound) load over the ice at speeds of up to 8 kph (5 mph). One dog acts as the leader: it takes its orders from the driver, and the other dogs follow the leader. There are three ways of hitching dogs to a sled: in the fan hitch each animal is attached by its own trace (lead); with two traces a team is harnessed in line between the traces; and with a single trace the lead dog is out in front with pairs of dogs hitched to the trace behind him. Other dogs used for sled work include the Alaskan Malemute, which many Arctic explorers have preferred to the Eskimo dog.

Large dogs used to be more extensively used to pull light carts, and they still perform this role in some parts of continental Europe.

More familiar to people in temperate lands are the working dogs which help to round up sheep and cattle. Although there are about ten recognised breeds of dogs which are classified as sheepdogs, the ones that actually do the work are Border Collies, lithe, intelligent black-and-white dogs with silky coats. There are many varieties of these useful animals, because the true Border Collie (if there ever was such a thing) has been crossed with other working breeds. They originated in England and have been exported all over the world. Almost every English farm has one or more dogs of the Border Collie type, but only the best are used by shepherds for the exacting task of herding sheep. The dog is controlled by the shepherd, usually by whistles. Different shouted or whistled commands tell it to stop, go right, go left, and go forward or back. A well-trained dog and its master can make a flock of sheep go exactly where they

Shepherd and sheepdog work closely together to manoeuvre sheep exactly where they want them to go. (Spectrum)

want them to. Australia has a strain of Cattle Dogs, bred from a mixture of Collie, Kelpie (an Australian sheepdog) and Dingo (the wild dog of Australia). These dogs work cattle, moving, like the Border Collies, in complete silence in response to commands from their masters.

An unusual job for which dogs are used is to hunt for truffles, delicious fungi which grow beneath the soil. Nondescript terriers are generally used for this purpose, though there used to be a breed called the Truffle Dog, which resembled a Poodle. In some parts people use pigs for truffle hunting.

Carrying messages is another job for which dogs have been used, but the supreme messengers are the homing or carrier pigeons. These birds fly back to their lofts when released at a distance, and can therefore be relied on to carry a message, written on rice paper and tied to one leg. Homing pigeons have been used for this purpose for at least 3000 years, for there are records of their work in ancient Egypt and Persia. How birds find their way over hundreds of kilometres of country is still a mystery, though modern research has proved that they have some way of navigating by means of the Sun and the stars. The pigeons fly at speeds between 50 and 100 kph (30-60 mph), and no wind, rain, or even fog can stop them. One interesting fact, however, is that there is a distance 'blind spot': a bird released up to 25 kilometres (15 miles) from home and one released more than 120 kilometres (75 miles) away will both find their way home with no apparent difficulty; but a bird released at a distance between those two points has difficulty in orientation.

A more modern application of animals to message carrying is currently under experiment in the US Navy. Naval scientists are training sea lions to carry messages to divers at depth up to 180 metres (100 fathoms). Under test the animals have been able to dive to these depths in about 2½ minutes — and unlike human divers they have no decompression problems.

Right: *When controlling crowds, a mounted policeman's superior height enables him to see and be seen easily.* (Spectrum)

Below: *A Californian sea lion being trained by the US Navy to carry messages to divers working under water.* (Rogers Color Lab. Corp.)

War
and Peacekeeping

The horse is a peaceful, vegetarian creature, even though individuals do show signs of vice from time to time. It is all the more shame, therefore, that for thousands of years they have been the backbone of the armies Man uses to fight his wars. Only in the past fifty years has the internal combustion engine taken over from animals, and with the known limit on fossil fuels there is a distinct danger that in the future animals may find themselves in the firing line again.

Of all the animals used in warfare, the horse is undoubtedly the most important. In open country, before the advent of firearms, a man on a horse had marked superiority over a man on foot. In a wooded or mountainous terrain the advantage went the other way, so from very early times cavalry and infantry each had a definite, comple-mentary role in warfare. The earliest cavalry were the warriors of the nomadic tribes of central Asia, which included the Huns and Mongols. Horses were part of their everyday life as they wandered from place to place over the plains, and they developed fast, strong hardy breeds suited as much to warfare as to travel.

Contact with the East gradually led to the introduction of cavalry into European armies. In the 300s BC King Philip of Macedon began the first systematic use of cavalry in a European force, having both light cavalry — lightly armed men on fast horses — for scouting, and heavy cavalry for charging the enemy. Philip's son, Alexander the Great, made great use of cavalry in his amazing conquests.

Cavalry continued to form part of the Greek armies, and was also used by the Romans, though only after they had suffered heavy defeats at the hands of armies with better cavalry than their own, such as the Carthaginian forces of Hannibal. The ratio of cavalry to infantry in these early armies seems to have been about 1:10. In Roman times one distinction between cavalry and infantry was that of class: then as now, a horse was an expensive item, and only the wealthier upper classes could afford

to be mounted in battle. This distinction continued right through the Middle Ages. One reason, too, was that the wealthier classes could afford body armour for protection, and since the weight of an armoured knight was roughly equivalent to that of a modern camper carrying knapsack and tent, the knight needed his horse as much as the camper needs to hitch a lift.

The development of armour, mostly chain-mail until after the Norman Conquest of England, and heavier plate armour in the later Middle Ages, led to the development of the so-called Great Horse, an animal big enough to bear the weight of man and metal — and even its own armour. Examination of armour shows that the stories of men in plate so heavy that they had to be winched on to their horses are apocryphal. Even

Top left: *This picture of the Charge of the Light Brigade during the Crimean War in 1854, shows the enormous numbers of animals employed in warfare in the past.* (Mary Evans Picture Library)

Above: *Museum dummies showing full body armour for horse and rider, as worn in the late 1400s.* (Mansell Collection)

Below left: *Up to the time of WWI training sessions like this were very important: an army riding school of about 1890.* (Mary Evans Picture Library)

tournament armour, which was always more heavily reinforced, was not so weighty that the wearer could not move freely. Also it must be remembered that men, and horses, were smaller in the Middle Ages, as proved by the heights of doors in old castles and the size of surviving suits of armour. Henry VIII, at 1.93 metres (6 feet 4 inches) tall, was a giant among his contemporaries. The Great Horse seems to have been a sturdy animal, around 1.5 metres high (15 hands), capable of a fast trot with an armoured man on its back.

Armour largely disappeared by the 17th century, except for breast and back plates. With it disappeared the Great Horse as a war horse, though its descendants survived to till the land. Lighter horses, sturdy but able to gallop in the charge, took its place, and continued as cavalry horses until recent times; indeed, the Russian army is still believed to have some cavalry regiments.

The continuing development of fire-power, particularly the machine-gun, made cavalry virtually useless by the time of World War I, but horses and other animals played a decisive part in that titanic struggle. The suffering and wastage were enormous. In the Boer War, fought under almost as difficult conditions some fifteen years earlier, the life of a horse was four months. Mules lasted a little longer, oxen, which pulled the guns, much less. Fever and exposure killed them off, not the bullets of the enemy. Josiah Wedgwood, a British politician and a member of the famous English pottery family, who served in that war, described in his memoirs having to put seventy-two of his own horses out of their misery. 'Once aboard the troop train,' he wrote, 'you found out that war was just — animals.' He spent his time looking after them, and found mules the most difficult: 'They dislike change, being conservative. If you want them to leave a truck they only bite you; if you want them to enter a truck, they kick. If you have never smelt a mule before, you wonder who was guilty of the invention'.

Actually, in the mud and appalling conditions of the Western Front in

Left: *Boer War scene: a British balloon corps on the march to Johannesburg. The balloon was used for reconnaissance.* (Mansell Collection)

Below: *Bringing up German artillery during one of the battles of World War I.* (Mary Evans Picture Library)

World War I, horses and mules were invaluable. Only they could struggle through the mud and slush into which rain and shelling turned the battle area, carrying supplies and drawing guns, taking reinforcements up to the front and the wounded back from it. The British army alone had more than a million horses and mules in action. By World War II the day of the war horse, whether as part of the cavalry or as a beast of burden, was well and truly over, and its place was taken by tanks and trucks, and by airborne men and supplies. Only in the US defence of the Philippines and in Russia were any cavalry used at all.

Of animals other than horses, mules have been used in warfare as beasts of burden, both for their hardiness and because they are sure-footed and can therefore carry loads in dangerous, mountain areas. Oxen and buffaloes were employed in India and other places to pull guns and supply wagons. Camels were naturally used by soldiers in desert places: Arab warriors themselves often rode horses, but their supplies came up by camel. The British Army, in the 19th century heyday of the British Empire, had a corps of soldiers riding camels, known as the camelry. The camel corps played an important part in the Sudan campaigns of the late 19th century, and

An Indian camel corps in a Republic Day parade in Delhi. (N.H.P.A.)

during World War I in the campaign against the Turks in Egypt. Many of the men and animals in the corps came from a corps maintained by the Indian Maharajah of Bikaner. Camels were widely used as supply animals in the Indian army.

In India, one of their native lands, elephants were used in warfare from very early times. They served as mobile strongpoints, covering the infantry, while bowmen from howdahs or castles on their backs discharged arrows at the enemy. The disadvantage was that the elephants sometimes bolted, and to stampede your enemy's elephants was a sure way to success in Indian warfare. Alexander the Great encountered elephants in the armies of the Persians, and later procured some from India for his own use. Thereafter they were increasingly used in the wars of western Asia among Alexander's successors: nearly 500 elephants are said to have taken part in the Battle of Ipsus (in what is now central Turkey) in 301 BC.

The Carthaginians adopted the idea of elephants as part of their war machine; possibly, like the Indians, they thought they would be of value as mobile battering rams to knock down the gates of besieged cities. In the First Punic War against Rome they deployed 100 elephants, and in the second, beginning in 218 BC, the Carthaginian general Hannibal took fifty elephants through Spain and over the Alpine passes to astonish the Roman soldiers on the plains of northern Italy. It is not certain whether Hannibal used African or Asian elephants, but the probability is that Asian elephants were employed. Elephants remained in use in India until the 19th century, and were even used to haul guns in the British Indian army.

A more pleasant chapter in the story of working animals is their role in peacekeeping. Horses are used for controlling traffic and crowds by the police forces of London, New York, Stockholm, Sydney and other cities. A policeman mounted on a 1.63 metres

Below: *Two mounted police officers in London. The city's Metropolitan Police Force is the oldest in the world to use mounted men.* (Spectrum)

Above: *Today horses play only a ceremonial part in the world's armies, such as this team drawing a gun-carriage.* (Spectrum)

Left: *A war elephant in action in 1858 during the Indian Mutiny.* (Mansell Collection)

Men of the Royal
Canadian Mounted Police
at a ceremonial parade.
Horses are no longer used
by the R.C.M.P. (Robert
Estall)

high (16 hands) horse has the great advantage that he can see over the heads of a crowd, and indeed over the top of many vehicles. The London Metropolitan Police maintain that in crowds a trained man on a trained horse can do the work of a dozen policemen on foot. Training a police horse takes about six months, sometimes more. During this time the horse is accustomed to the noise and bustle of crowds, traffic, trains and even low-flying aircraft, and learns to obey the slightest command of its rider. Horses begin training at the age of three or four years, and have a working life of around fourteen years. The

Metropolitan Police horses have a long history, beginning in 1758 when 'two persuit horses and proper persuers' were attached to the office of the magistrate Sir John Fielding at Bow Street court.

The mounted law officers — sheriffs and marshals — of America's Wild West are now legendary, but they were none-the-less real for all that. Equally famous, and roughly contemporary, were the first 'Mounties', the North-West Mounted Police founded in Canada in 1873, known since 1920 as the Royal Canadian Mounted Police. The Mounties gave up their horses in the late 1960s, except for ceremonial purposes.

Right: *Show jumping has become an increasingly popular sport, partly because of its frequent appearance on television.* (Spectrum)

Sport
and Entertainment

Although sport and entertainment are fun for most of the people watching, they are work, hard and skilled work, for those taking part and for the animals which are involved. Most modern sports had their origin in games designed to make people fit for warfare — lacrosse, an American Indian war game, is a case in point — and sports involving animals are no exception. This is particularly true of what has been called 'the sport of kings': horse-racing in all its many forms. For example, Xenophon, living in Greece in the 300s BC, trained warriors in cross-country riding, the direct ancestor of our modern steeplechase.

Horse-racing as we know it today was developed under the patronage of the Stuart kings of England, particularly James I and his grandson, Charles II. They helped to improve the stock, and imported Arabian horses into England for breeding. The last of the Stuart monarchs, Queen Anne, founded Ascot racecourse.

The pre-eminent horse in the racing world is the English Thoroughbred, now classified as a distinct breed. Without exception, all the Thoroughbreds the world over are descended from just three stallions, imported into England more than 250 years ago. These stallions were the Byerly Turk, who arrived in Britain just before 1690; the Darley Arabian, imported from Syria in 1704; and the Godolphin Arabian, imported from France around 1730. In each line the descent has come through just one descendant of these three horses: Herod (the Byerly), Eclipse (the Darley), and Matchem (the Godolphin). The three original Arabians were mated with English-bred mares, which may have had some Arabian blood in them. The result is a delicate but elegant horse, capable of very fast speeds over varying distances. The breeding of racehorses is now big business, the principal breeding

Horse racing is probably the most popular of all the sports involving animals, in all parts of the world. (N.H.P.A., James Tallon)

countries being Britain, Ireland, France, Italy, the United States and Canada, Australia, New Zealand, Argentina and Chile.

There are thousands of different races every year, but a handful have become known as 'classics' and victory in them is a matter of prestige for horse, jockey, breeder and owner. The main classic races include: in England, the St. Leger, the Derby, the Oaks, the 2000 Guineas and the 1000 Guineas; in the United States, the Kentucky Derby, the Preakness Stakes and the Belmont Stakes; in Australia, the Melbourne Cup; in France, the Prix de l'Arc de Triomphe, the Prix du Jockey Club and the Grand Prix de Paris.

All these races are flat races, but equally important are the races colloquially known as 'over the sticks', the various steeplechase and hurdles races. Steeplechasing gets its name from informal cross-country races among huntsmen in England from a time when the objective was to reach the next church steeple. Steeplechasing is particularly popular in France and the United States, but the world's most famous steeplechase is the Grand National in England. As popular in the United States and France, and in the Soviet Union too, are trotting and pacing races, in which the racing horse pulls a light cart. Such harness races are the direct descendants of the chariot races of ancient Rome. The two kinds of harness horses are trotters and pacers. The trotter moves diagonally-opposite legs together; the pacer moves the legs on each side together. Both kinds of horses are evolved from Thoroughbred stock, but in the United States a completely fresh breed has been made known as the Standardbred. Almost all Standardbreds are descended from a stallion named Hambletonian, himself a descendant of the Darley Arabian.

Harness racing, in which horses pull small two-wheeled carts called sulkies, is a popular sport in Malta, where this race was photographed, and in North America, Australia, France, Italy, New Zealand and Sweden. (Spectrum)

The National Hunt Steeplechase at Cheltenham, England. Primarily a British sport, steeplechasing has grown in popularity around Europe, Canada, USA, Australia and New Zealand. (Colorsport)

Far right: *An unusual form of racing, using ostriches as the mounts! This race was held at Oudtshoorn, in Cape Province, South Africa, centre for ostrich farming.* (ZEFA, V Phillips)

Right: *Horses are often used by holiday-makers for cross-country exploration — trail riding in North America, or pony-trekking in Britain. Here a group of riders are exploring an Arizona parkland.* (N.H.P.A., James Tallon)

Top: *Camel racing has long been a popular sport in Arab countries, using the fleet-footed Dromedaries, or Arabian racing camels. A Dromedary with one rider can travel as much as 190 kilometres (120 miles) in a day. This race was held in Bahrain.* (Spectrum)

Right: *Rodeos, contests reviving the skills of the Wild West, are popular in Canada and the United States. A feature of these contests is a chuck-wagon race, a chuck-wagon being a cowboy's mobile kitchen.* (Spectrum)

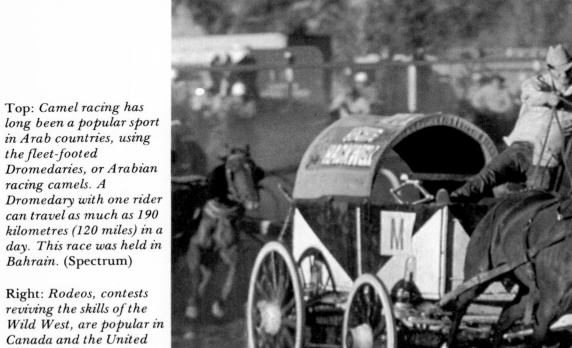

Hunting on horseback tends to be in pursuit of foxes, deer or hares. The hunter is generally a Thoroughbred or a cross between a Thoroughbred and a more substantial breed; the average hunter has to carry a much heavier rider than a racehorse, and over rough country. Fox hunting began in England around the mid 1600s, and was taken to North America by English colonists. American country generally needs heavier horses than the English countryside.

Fox hunting is one of the main sports using dogs. The English Foxhound, a small, compact animal with a keen nose, has been specially bred for the sport. American Foxhounds are more diverse in size and shape, and are used for other kinds of sport besides foxes. Both these breeds are members of the much larger hound group, some of which hunt by scent, and others by sight. For example, Beagles are used to hunt hares by scent, while Greyhounds and Whippets hunt by sight in the sport known as coursing. Over the years dogs have been bred for particular quarry: Badgers — Dachshunds (which means badger dogs); Wolves — Irish Wolfhounds, Weimeraners and Borzois; Gazelles — Afghans and Salukis; and a group of dogs whose names indicate their prey — Elkhounds, Otterhounds, Coonhounds and Deerhounds. Terriers, as a group, are — or were — also used for hunting, particularly vermin such as rats, and for flushing out foxes for the hounds to chase. Many breeds of Terriers began their existence as working dogs, and some still are used for that purpose. A lot of these working Terriers are cross-bred animals.

Left: *Fox-hunting was started in England in the 1700s, and spread to North America. Fox-hounds are specially bred for the sport, and the horses are generally Thoroughbreds crossed with heavier working horses.* (Spectrum)

Top right: *Beagles are smaller than fox-hounds, and are used for hunting hares and rabbits. They are followed on foot.* (N.H.P.A., J Good)

Page 63, bottom right: *Slipping a Greyhound for coursing, that is, releasing it to pursue the hare. Borzois, Deerhounds and Salukis are also used for coursing.* (Spectrum)

Left: *One of the oldest breeds of dog in the world, Greyhounds are also the fastest. The first mention of an actual race appeared in the London* Times *as early as 1876.* (Colorsport)

The sport of coursing hares has given rise to another sport: Greyhound racing. In this the Greyhounds race round an oval track in pursuit of an electric 'hare'. Dog racing began in the United States in 1919, and quickly spread to Britain, where it is still popular. Whippets are sometimes raced in this way.

The other big group of sporting dogs comprises the gundogs, which are used by sportsmen shooting game, mostly birds. These dogs are of many breeds, and are divided according to the kind of work they do. Pointers and Setters pick up the position of game by sniffing the air. The Pointers stiffen and literally point towards the birds they have scented, with tail, nose and body in a straight line. Setters also point, but sometimes crouch down and creep up on the quarry. At one time both Pointers and Setters were expected to retrieve birds that had been shot, but in the early 1800s breeders began to produce Retrievers for this work. Golden Retrievers and Labradors are the most popular breeds, while in the United States the Chesapeake Bay Retriever, which has a thick, oily waterproof coat, is unrivalled for fetching duck in cold water. Spaniels, of which there are many kinds, are used to work through the undergrowth flushing out birds for the guns, and retrieving them when shot.

Above: *A Brittany Spaniel bringing its master a quail which it has retrieved. This breed is popular in France and the United States as a game dog.* (N.H.P.A., James Tallon)

Left: *Terrier racing is a country sport popular in some parts of Britain. The dogs here are small, short-legged terriers known as Jack Russells — not a recognised breed.* (Spectrum)

Right: *A Chesapeake Bay Retriever, one of the best dogs for duck hunting in the United States, looking for a bird that has fallen in the water.* (N.H.P.A., J Good)

Below: *Returning with the bag — a pointer with a pheasant.* (ARDEA)

Some other animals are used much like dogs for hunting. The most exotic is probably the Cheetah, a large animal of the cat family which is native to Asia and Africa. It is also the fastest runner over short distances, and can reach speeds up to 110 kph (70 mph). Cheetahs have been domesticated in several Asian countries, particularly India and Persia (modern Iran), and trained to chase and catch game such as deer. The Ferret, a domestic form of the Weasel, is used to drive rats and rabbits out of their holes. Ferrets are generally worked in pairs, a male and a female. The female is kept in a bag at ground level while her mate goes down the hole; her calling helps to coax the male back to the surface when he might wish to linger over a tasty meal of rabbit.

Several kinds of birds are used for sport. The racing of homing Pigeons is popular in Europe and North America, and Pigeon fanciers spend a great deal of time and money in breeding and training champion birds. In the Far East some people use Cormorants for fishing. These web-footed birds dive under water in pursuit of fish, and can stay submerged for an amazingly long time. A fisherman using a Cormorant takes it out in a boat, and attaches a ring or harness around the bird's long neck to prevent it from swallowing any fish it catches. A cord attached to the harness prevents the bird from flying away.

However, the main form of bird sport is falconry, also known as hawking. It is a very old sport, and was known in ancient China and Persia around 4000 years ago. Two kinds of birds of prey, Falcons and Hawks, are used, and are

Left: *The characteristic pose of a pointer at work, pointing to game with tail and head in a straight line.* (Sally Anne Thompson)

Top right: *A Bedouin falconer with his hawk, hooded and sitting on his padded arm, in Qatar. Falconry is very popular in Arab countries.* (Spectrum, M Ericson)

Bottom right: *An American kestrel — sometimes called a sparrow hawk — on a hunting perch.* (Animals Animals)

indeed the only species that can be trained. Long-winged birds, known as 'Hawks of the lure', include Peregrine Falcons (the most popular), the Northern Falcon and the Iceland Gyrfalcon. Short-winged Hawks, known as 'Hawks of the fist', are the Goshawk and Sparrowhawk.

Hawking was, like horseracing, the sport of kings, and it was a favourite sport of two great English monarchs, Harold II, the last of the Saxons, and Elizabeth I. Like so many ancient sports it has a language all its own. Female birds, which are preferred for the sport, are called falcons, while the smaller males are known as tercels. A fledgling taken from the nest is an eyas, and it is generally the best bird to train; an immature bird taken in flight is a passager, while an untamed adult is a haggard. Training takes time and patience. First, the bird must be manned — that is, accustomed to the presence of people. It must then be accustomed to wearing a hood, often called a rufter-hood, which covers its eyes. While hooded the bird is docile, and can be accustomed to perch on the falconer's heavily-gloved wrist. Around the bird's legs are short strips of leather known as jesses, with a bell just above each jess. The sound of the bell tells the falconer where his bird has gone when it has flown out of sight. A leash is attached to the jesses and is held in the hand while the bird is being trained by use of the lure. A lure consists of a weight covered with feathers and with food tied to it. The lure, which has strings attached, is thrown, and the hawk is taught to fly to the lure and grasp it.

Hawks are used for catching and killing various kinds of game birds, such as Grouse, Partridge and Woodcock, and also for Hares and Rabbits. In Asia Bustards and Ducks are also hunted. Falconry today is practised in Britain, the United States, France, Germany, Austria, India, Pakistan and the Arab countries.

Closely allied to sport is the use of animals for entertainment, and it is often difficult to say where the border between the two categories lies. One group of sports has very little that is sporting about it, and is designed mainly for the entertainment of spectators. It involves fighting, either between men and animals, or among animals themselves. As part of their public games the Romans relished the sport of *venationes*, hunting wild animals for public amusement, generally in the arena. The men pitted against the animals were often condemned criminals or prisoners of war. When Nero and other emperors persecuted Christians, many of those unfortunates, men and women alike, were put into the arena with lions and other wild beasts and left to fend for themselves unarmed. Thousands of animals were killed at the opening of the Colosseum in Rome in AD 80.

Cruel sports of a later date included bearbaiting with dogs, popular in London from the 10th century onwards (it was prohibited in 1835); badger baiting, also using dogs; and cockfighting. In this last sport two specially bred gamecocks fight each other to the death. It is still popular in Spain, Latin America and parts of Asia, and is secretly practised in many countries such as the United States and Britain where it has been outlawed.

Below: *An Iban boy of south-western Borneo with a fighting cock. The sport, illegal in Britain and most parts of North America, is still popular in many countries.* (S C Bisserot)

The most important of the present-day spectator sports which involve the killing of animals is bullfighting, the national sport of Spain. It is essentially a spectacle for the audience and has a long history. In ancient Crete, 4000 years ago, a form of bullbaiting was practised, which may have had a religious significance: the religion of Crete was based on the legend of the Minotaur, a monster which was reputed to be half bull, half man. The bulls used in modern bullfighting are specially bred to be fierce and dangerous.

An afternoon's performance in a bullring is known as a corrida, and the men taking part (sometimes a few women as well) are the toreros, or bullmen. Each bull is killed in a ballet-like ritual, which the spectators find all the more exciting because of the very real danger involved. The toreros include picadors, mounted horsemen who pierce the bull with lances to try to weaken its neck muscles. Their horses are usually well padded, though until this horn-proof armour was introduced in the 1930s the mortality among the horses was considerable — and painful. Then come the banderilleros, foot-fighters who plant darts in the animal's neck. Finally the star of the show, the matador, enters, and plays the animal with his cape. The cape is red, but since the bull is colour-blind the colour is not important. After displaying his courage and skill sufficiently, the matador kills the bull with his sword. Many matadors have lost their lives in this dangerous activity.

The Spanish form of bullfighting is popular in several Spanish-American countries, but in Portugal the bull's horns are padded and few animals are actually killed. In the Camargue, part of France lying between the two arms of the Rhône River, the razeteurs, or bullfighters, spend their time trying to take cockades or ribbons tied to the bull's horns, and the bull is not killed, although a few Provençal cities have bullfights in the Spanish style.

Right: *Bullfighting in the Camargue, in southern France. A mounted contestant dodges the bull's charge, having snatched the ribbons from its horns.* (Spectrum)

While the modern bullfight could be viewed as the descendant of the uglier aspects of Roman circuses, modern circuses show animals in far more pleasant ways. Circus horses are trained to respond to their riders in a way few horses do outside the ring, and to pad steadily round the ring while a rider performs balancing feats. Some horses perform evolutions and 'dance' apparently in time to music, but actually the conductor of the circus orchestra watches the horses and times his players to follow the performers! Signals to the horses are often given by the cracking of a whip, which has led to many stories of cruelty in the ring. In the best circuses such stories are untrue, because no trainer could get a really good performance from an animal that was ill-treated. Circus animals are always kept in the pink of condition, and

Bertram Mills' Circus, famous in the 1930s and 40s in England, used to invite spectators to view the animals in their quarters after each performance.

An amazing variety of animals are trained to perform in the circus, and their acts are a tribute to the skill of the trainer — and sometimes, when naturally fierce animals such as tigers, lions and bears are involved, to the trainer's courage too. Besides the animals already named, elephants, dogs, monkeys, birds, sealions and snakes are used in circus acts.

Similar skilled training is needed for animals that perform on stage and screen. Dogs and horses are the favourite animals for this purpose. Among the most famous film stars of the animal world have been Champion the wonder horse, Roy Rogers's horse Trigger, and Lassie, dog heroine of many movies. In

at least some films the part of Lassie is said to have been a drag act, performed by a male dog.

Among the most intelligent animals are dolphins, and in recent years many of these lively creatures have been kept in dolphinariums, where they are taught to jump through hoops, fetch balls and other objects, and jump high in the air for fish.

Left: *Lassie has been the heroine of many animal films. Several Collie dogs, male and female, have played the rôle.* (Kobal Collection)

Below: *Dolphins can be trained to do many tricks. This animal at Ocean World, Fort Lauderdale, Florida, is leaping over a high line. Dolphins also jump through hoops and can catch and throw a ball.* (Heather Angel)

Far left: *Animals form a basic part of the circus.* (Spectrum)

Left: *Roy Rogers' horse Trigger, a golden Palomino, was one of the best-known of animal film stars.* (Kobal Collection)

Finally, there is a group of sports-cum-entertainments involving horses. This group includes polo, a ball-game played by mounted men riding polo ponies. These ponies are generally of racehorse or hunter stock, and are not ponies (small horses) at all. The game originated in Persia, probably some time before 500 BC. A well-trained polo pony enters into the spirit of the game every bit as much as its rider, and can position itself to give the rider the best possible shot at the ball. The other form of show sport is often given the general name of eventing, and it is a competition which includes three tests of the skill of both riders and horses. The first part is dressage, in which horse and rider show off their paces in the show ring, generally over a figure-of-eight or more complicated course. This exercise demands complete control by the rider and a good understanding on the part of the horse. Only a well-trained horse can excel in dressage. The second part of eventing is cross-country riding, which requires very different qualities from the same rider and horse. In the cross-country the horse and rider must cover a demanding course containing many fearsome obstacles, with points deducted for loss of time.

The final part of an event is show-jumping, often held as a competitive event by itself. In this trial, horse and rider have to negotiate a series of formidable jumps in the show-ring; however, the jumps are constructed in such a way that they collapse if a horse fails to clear them, and injuries are few. Show-jumping has become internationally popular in the past thirty or so years, helped by television.

Top left: *Polo ponies become as skilful at the game as their riders, and know exactly how to place themselves for a winning hit.* (Spectrum)

Opposite: *Show jumping has become an increasingly popular sport, partly because of its frequent appearance on television.* (Spectrum)

Guides
and Protectors

Animals play a very large part in our lives as guides and protectors, a role in which they are perhaps less often seen than the animals which do hard physical work or provide entertainment. As guides and protectors dogs are the most useful and important animals, and nowhere is this more evident than in the work they do for blind people.

Dogs have led blind people around for hundreds, perhaps thousands, of years, but the highly-trained guide dogs of today are a modern development. The guide dog movement began in Germany during World War I. A doctor treating war wounded in 1916 found that his German shepherd (Alsatian) dog was so helpful to a blinded soldier that he began to train dogs to guide those who had lost their sight. From Germany the guide dog movement spread to the United States in the early 1920s, and to Britain in the early 1930s. It has now spread to many other countries in Europe and elsewhere, including Australia and South Africa.

The most popular breed for use as guide dogs is the Labrador Retriever, and about 70 per cent of all guide dogs are Labradors. The rest are German shepherds, Golden retrievers and cross-breeds. Size is important: a guide dog must be not less than 48 centimetres (19 inches) high at the shoulder, though a very short person could use a smaller dog, and a very tall man or woman would need a larger dog. Bitches are preferred to dogs for the work, partly because the males' natural territorial instincts make them less suitable. Temperament plays a very large part in the selection of guide dogs. The dog must not be nervous or aggressive, and must have a genuine desire to please. The training period reveals any defect in the dog's character, and rather more than one-third of all dogs initially selected for training fail to meet all the requirements.

The various guide dog associations tend to breed their own dogs in order to ensure that as high a proportion as possible is suitable for training. However, life in kennels is not a good preparation for a guide dog's eventual life in somebody's home, so from the age of eight weeks the puppies are sent to foster homes for nine months' preliminary training. The puppy-walkers, as the foster owners are known, concentrate on house training, teaching the puppy to walk on the lead, and getting it used to the sound of traffic and visiting such places as shops, restaurants, and places with lifts.

Training proper lasts between six and eight months. The dog is taught to wear harness, to obey certain commands, and to walk just in front and to the left of the handler. Then comes the most difficult part of the training — learning how to negotiate obstacles while leaving enough room for the handler, and how to deal with traffic. Because traffic sense is vital, training is always done in busy towns.

Page 75: *St. Bernard dogs have a fine record of saving lives in the Alps, though the brandy cask is a bit of modern show-manship.* (Sally Anne Thompson)

Below: *A guide dog leads its owner along a pavement. The dog walks on the blind person's left; here it is checking that the entrance way is clear before proceeding.* (ZEFA)

The dog is taught to stop at the edge of the footpath, and not to proceed until given the command 'Forward'. It has to ignore even this command until it is safe to cross the road. Guide dogs quickly learn to recognise and use pedestrian crossings, because they see other people using them.

Once the dog is trained, the animal's new owner has to be trained, too. Not all blind people can make use of guide dogs, because of age or physical disability, including deafness. The training course takes four weeks, during which time the blind person and the dog get to know each other and to work together. Regular after-care visits by trainers help to solve any problems once the blind person and the dog have settled down. The partnership lasts for an average of eight or nine years, though some dogs can carry on working for as long as twelve years. At the end of its working life the dog generally becomes just a family pet, and a new guide dog is provided. Guide dogs allow the blind a degree of freedom and independence which sighted persons find hard to realise.

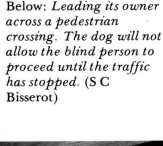

Below: *Leading its owner across a pedestrian crossing. The dog will not allow the blind person to proceed until the traffic has stopped.* (S C Bisserot)

A far longer story of guiding and service is that of the St. Bernard dog, one of the largest breeds. These dogs were bred by the monks at the hospice, or house of entertainment for strangers, at the Swiss side of the Great St. Bernard Pass in the Alps. The hospice was founded more than 900 years ago by St. Bernard of Menthon, or Montjoux, who as archdeacon of Aosta had the responsibility for the welfare of travellers in the Alps. The hospice stands at the highest point in the pass, and is staffed by Augustinian monks, all young, fit men and excellent skiers and mountaineers. For hundreds of years they have bred the great dogs which bear the name of the hospice to help them in rescuing foot travellers trapped in the snow. The dog's size and strength and its keen sense of smell make it particularly suited for the work. Having located an injured or stranded person, the dog signals for help by barking. The most famous St. Bernard was 'Barry', which saved more than forty lives before losing its own. The St. Bernards also acted as Alpine guide dogs, steering voyagers over dangerous trails through the mountains. Although the St. Bernard is often shown with a small keg of brandy suspended from its collar, this romantic touch was, alas, the invention of the English artist Sir Edwin Landseer.

Today also other breeds of dogs, particularly German shepherd dogs, are used in mountain rescue work and are trained to find people buried under avalanches. The use of helicopters has helped to reduce the dependence on dogs for Alpine rescue.

For thousands of years man has depended on dogs for security, probably ever since a cave man's pet growled to warn of the approach of wolves. Today millions of households keep dogs in the dual roles of pets and guards, but the

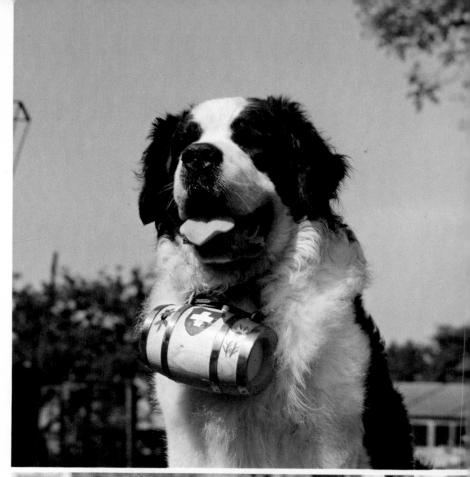

Above right: St. Bernard dogs have a fine record of saving lives in the Alps, though the brandy cask is a bit of modern showmanship. (Sally Anne Thompson)

Right: German shepherd dogs (Alsations) make excellent guard dogs; here, one is protecting a barge. (Spectrum)

security services employ specially selected and trained animals to help patrol streets and buildings. The police have a long tradition of using dogs, and in England parish constables patrolled with dogs as early as the 1400s. The use of dogs as active members of police forces developed in continental Europe in the early years of the 20th century and was taken up by the British police in the 1940s, after the end of World War II. As with guide dogs, temperament is important in police work, though a somewhat different nature is required. The most popular dog for police work is the highly intelligent German shepherd dog which is easily trained, and can look — and be — extremely fierce when necessary. Other dogs used by police forces, both in Europe and elsewhere, include Airedales, Boxers, Dobermann pinschers, Rottweilers and Weimaraners. In addition some Labradors are used, especially for detecting drugs and explosives.

A police dog is allocated to a handler — a serving policeman — as a puppy, and is partly trained by him. At the age of a year the dog begins an intensive twelve-week training course, in which it is taught to follow scent across various kinds of country, to search a wide variety of places, including buildings, for particular people or property, and to bark when it is successful. The dog is also trained to chase after a runaway and to hold him. It does this by circling the criminal if he stands still, barking to call its handler, but if the criminal continues to run the dog seizes him by the right arm, being careful not to bite. To keep dog and handler up to the mark they attend frequent refresher training courses.

A police dog and its handler do an eight-hour day, of which seven hours are spent on patrol. This work may entail up to 40 kilometres (25 miles) walking. If most of this is over hard city pavements the dog's working life is shortened,

Below right: *In training, police dogs have to be able to clear high obstacles, so that they can readily pursue suspects.* (ZEFA, Kurt Scholz)

because too much road work is bad for the feet. The average working life of a police dog is six years, but it may be less if its patrolling is mostly on roads. Dogs are often taken to the scene of their work by van, thus making the dog patrols highly mobile. The remaining on-duty time is taken up with grooming and feeding.

Other security forces which use dogs include the US coastguard, and also the many private security firms which guard factories and other premises at night. A specialised form of patrol work is carried out by dogs attached to police of the armed services — army, navy and air force. In Britain the Royal Air Force Police School at Newton, near Nottingham, has one of the world's leading dog training schools. There the RAF trains dogs not only for its own use, but for the police, the customs and excise service, the navy, and the American forces in Europe.

Left: *Up and over a high ladder — part of the rigorous training given to dogs at the R.A.F. Police School at Newton, Nottinghamshire.* (Spectrum)

Top right: *Because they may have to tackle any kind of situation, police dogs are trained to go through fire jumps.* (Spectrum)

Right: *A police dog in training hitches a lift on its coach's back.* (Spectrum)

The British Customs and Excise service introduced a special corps of drug detector dogs in 1978. The dogs, trained by the RAF, are experts at sniffing out cannabis and heroin, and their handlers include three women; the service is believed to be the first in the world to use women handlers in drug detection. The dogs used are Labradors and other breeds of retrievers, which have especially sensitive noses. They work at ports, airports and inland container depots. They are used to check baggage, though not in the presence of passengers. Customs departments of other countries used dogs for drug sniffing long before this, and had some successes, although sometimes the dogs did make mistakes. One French Customs dog sniffed a car enthusiastically for drugs (there were none in it), and eventually bounded triumphantly to its handler, bearing a rather stale egg and cress sandwich. It is not surprising that training programmes demand a very high standard, and only three in every hundred dogs successfully complete the course. Precautions are taken to make sure that the dogs themselves do not get 'hooked' on the drugs they are seeking.

After sniffing an article of clothing, a Bloodhound can follow the scent for very considerable distances — a valuable trait when tracking missing or 'wanted' people. (Sally Anne Thompson)

Even more specialised than the dogs which seek drugs are those which hunt for concealed explosives. Those used include Labradors, German shepherds, Golden retrievers, Pointers, and Münsterlanders (black-and-white multi-purpose gundogs, bred from hawking dogs and land spaniels), but the individual dog matters much more than the breed, and dogs of many other retrieving breeds have been tried successfully.

One breed of dog that has traditionally been used for tracking for hundreds of years — ever since Roman times — is the mournful-looking bloodhound, formerly known also as the sleuth-hound. Bloodhounds have extremely sensitive noses, and their name comes from the persistence with which they can follow the trail of blood, even if it is several hours old. Because of the spread of civilization there is much less open country today, and so bloodhounds are of little value in finding people, despite the popular image of them as man-trackers. In the days of slavery in the United States a variety of bloodhound known as a Cuban hound was used for hunting down runaway slaves. It looked like a cross between a bulldog and a mastiff, and was renowned for its ferocity, whereas the true bloodhound is a gentle animal.

Many dogs are used to give warning of the approach of strangers or unwanted intruders, but dogs are not the only animals that serve man in this way. Geese have a good record for giving the alarm, the most famous occasion being the siege of Rome by the Gauls in 390 BC. After prolonged fighting the Romans were forced back to their last fortress, the strong-walled Capitol. The Gauls mounted a night attack which might have succeeded but for the noise made by the sacred geese in the Temple of Juno, which aroused one of the commanders, Marcus Manlius, in time to repulse the assault.

Geese are aggressive birds, and will make a fuss at the arrival of an intruder. (Bruce Coleman)

A different form of security is provided the world over by cats, which are kept on farms and in stores and factories to hunt and kill mice and rats. The domestic cat is a natural predator, and is probably the most independent of all the animals man has domesticated. Though many pet-food pampered pussies might merely blink if faced by a mouse, a good working cat kept for mousing will more than justify its existence in a year's hunting. In countries such as India where snakes are a problem many people keep mongooses, animals which move so fast that they can even kill poisonous snakes such as cobras. They grip them just below the head before the reptiles have time to strike. A mongoose is also a good ratter, and many were imported into Hawaii and parts of the West Indies to deal with plagues of rats there.

Right: *Guinea pigs are greatly valued for biological and medical research, because they are easy to rear and breed freely — two or three times a year.* (Animals Animals)

Left: *The ordinary domestic puss plays an important part in guarding its home against vermin.* (Spectrum)

Research
and Medicine

Millions of people are alive and well today who would be dead if it were not for the part played by animals in medical research. This is a very sensitive subject on which people hold conflicting views, but there is no doubt of the benefits which animals have conferred on mankind through their use in experiments. Many countries have protective legislation which controls who carries out the experiments, the nature of the experiments, and the care of the animals before, during and after the tests or other activities.

Some research with animals is largely dependent on a study of their normal behaviour, and does not bring them within the category of animal workers. However, a great deal of our knowledge about the working of the brain has been derived from experiments in which animals have been set tasks, and the ways in which they solve them have been carefully noted. Such experiments are carried out with rather more knowledge and with less likelihood of harm to the animal than those made by that gentle English cleric, Gilbert White of

Left and right: *The Pig-tailed Macaque Monkey can be trained to climb palm trees and throw down coconuts to its owner. These animals help in botanical research, and in Malaysia they have been employed to collect specimens from tall trees.* (N.H.P.A., Ivan Polunin)

Selborne, on his tortoise Timothy. White's journal entry, dated July 1, 1780 reads: 'We put Timothy into a tub of water, and found that he sunk gradually, and walked on the bottom of the tub: he seemed quite out of his element, and was much dismayed. This species seems not at all amphibious.' Fortunately Timothy survived for many years thereafter.

Rats are particularly favoured for behavioural experiments and for tests involving their capacity to learn. Such animals are bred especially for their laboratory work and are kept in clean and comfortable conditions: these are essential because otherwise the scientists conducting the experiments would not get a true picture of the animals' responses. The kinds of experiments include finding the way through a maze to a reward in the shape of a titbit of food, and operating various simple kinds of mechanisms which also produce food. One of the pioneers of this kind of research was the Russian physicist, Ivan Pavlov (1849-1936). Some of Pavlov's most important work was on the subject of conditioned reflexes — automatic but induced responses to stimulation. Using dogs, he found that not only does a dog's mouth water when food is put into it, but that if a bell is rung every time the food is produced, after a while the dog's mouth waters as soon as it hears the bell, even if no food appears.

Apart from the use of animals in developing new techniques in surgery — we owe most of our modern heart surgery, including all the transplant techniques, to this sort of experimentation — an important field of research is in the testing of new drugs, to ensure that the side effects from taking them are not harmful. Indeed, production batches of some drugs must be tested similarly to ensure that no deleterious properties have crept in during routine manufacture. Animals employed for this testing include cats,

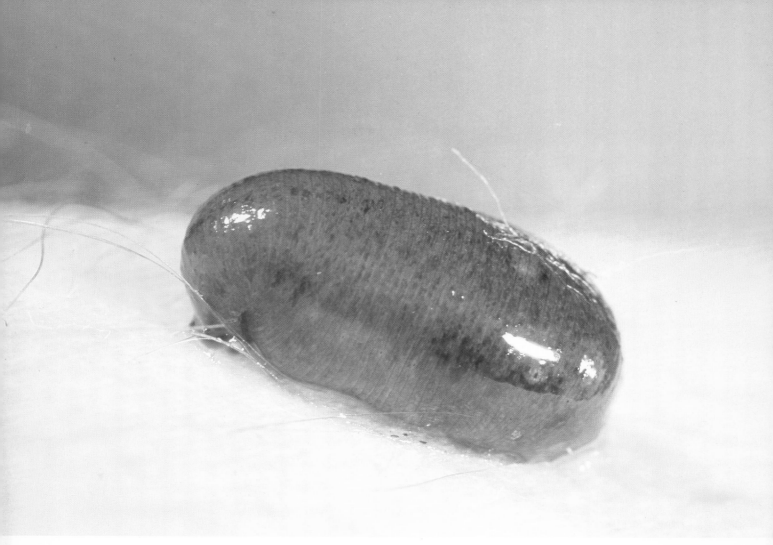

Above: *A leech feeding on blood from a man's arm. At one time leeches were commonly used to let blood from patients.* (Oxford Scientific Films)

Overleaf: *A pigeon being trained to get food from a machine. Research into animal behaviour of this kind is valuable in the study of reflexes and the function of the brain.* (Oxford Scientific Films)

chickens, dogs, mice, rats and rabbits. Monkeys, which in their physiology are nearer to humans than most other animals, are also used in drug testing.

Animals were the first living creatures to fly and to travel in space. In 1783 the pioneer balloon-makers Joseph and Jacques Montgolfier sent a duck, a rooster and a sheep on an eight-minute flight in one of their early balloons. The animals landed safely, and a month later a man, the historian Jean Pilâtre de Rozier, followed their example. On November 3, 1957, the Russians sent their second spacecraft, *Sputnik 2,* into orbit around the Earth, just a month after the launch of the first-ever spacecraft, *Sputnik 1.* The first *Sputnik* was unmanned, but *Sputnik 2* carried a passenger, a small dog named Laika. Laika did not return safely to Earth, but before the flight ended it was fed a drugged piece of food to ensure a quick and painless death.

In a later space experiment US astronauts took some spiders with them on a space flight, to see how the animals would react to weightlessness. Astronauts have found that the absence of gravity makes many apparently simple tasks difficult, even moving about. One of the spiders, called Arabella, managed to make a web, a very erratic one indeed, but a second web completed a few days later when it was more accustomed to the absence of gravity was much more like those webs that spiders spin on Earth.

Other uses of animals in medicine include the employment of leeches to suck blood, in the days when blood-letting was a popular remedy for many ills. The kind of leech used was the medicinal leech, *Hirudo medicinalis.* The leech produces a substance called hirudin, which prevents blood from clotting. Maggots have been used to clear up bacterial infection in a wound,

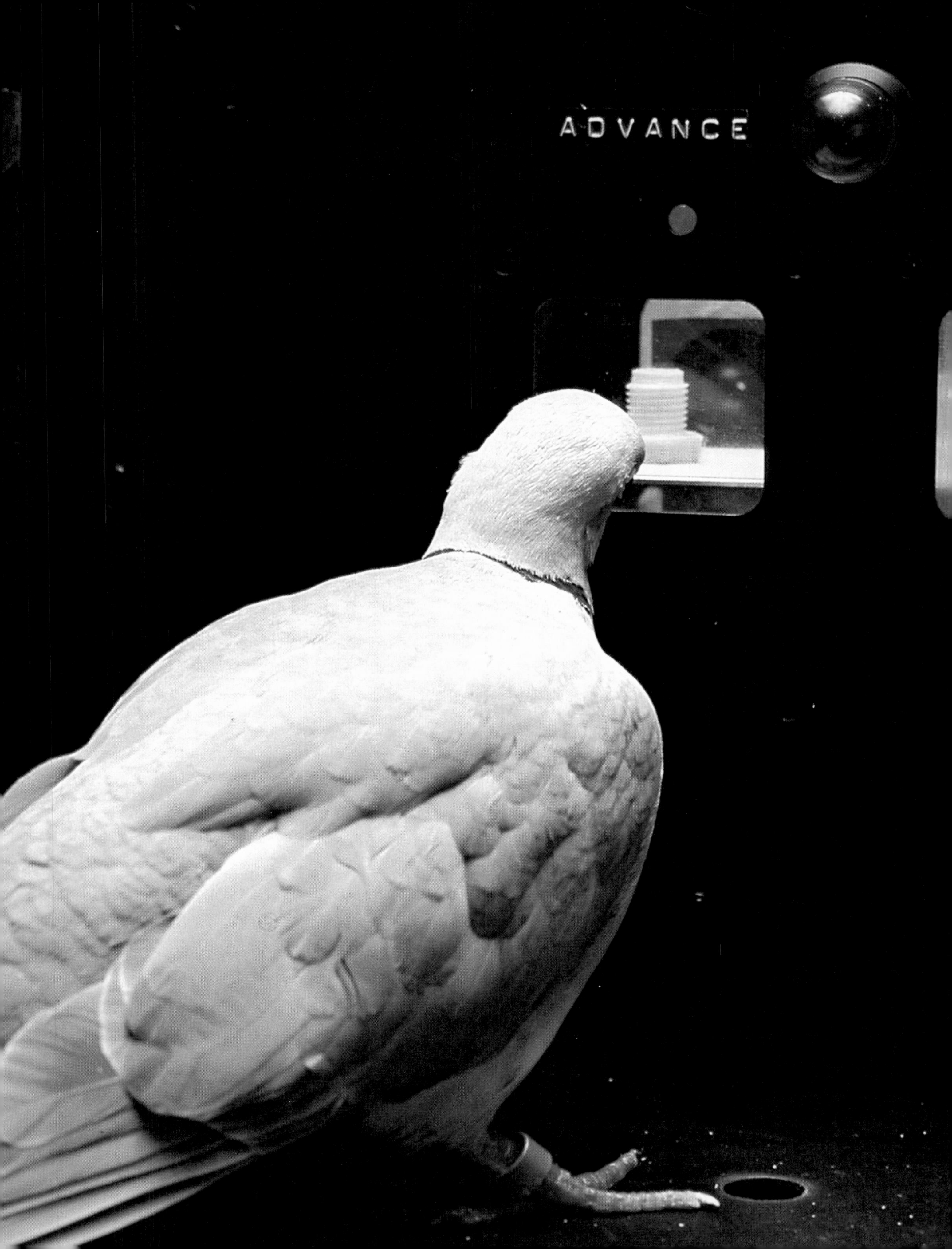
ADVANCE

and certain kinds of ants have been incited to clip the edges of surgical incisions together with their pincers. However, these three examples are probably instances of animals doing what comes naturally, even while working for Man.

Humans owe a great deal to the animals with which they share their lives. More and more people are beginning to realise this, and indeed there is the distinct possibility of a return to the use of animals, particularly on the land. When the world's supplies of oil run out, or the fossil fuels become too expensive to use, farmers may well have to turn again to the great horses which our grandparents used. A well-kept Shire horse has a longer working life than any tractor, and the animal puts something back into the ground in the form of valuable manure, as well as taking out its food.

It has been demonstrated that, except in bad conditions, animals benefit from working, just as humans do, and that an animal that has a job to do and does it well is a happy one. Nobody, for example, ever sees a healthy working sheepdog looking discontented or fretful. There is a lesson for us in this, that even when we keep animals as pets they should have something stimulating to do, even if it is only going through obedience tests. This kind of occupation provides interest for dogs in particular. A point to remember is that we cannot expect work from our animals unless we work with them.

Below: *Even the humble woodlouse is used for behavioural experiments, which eventually help ecologists to understand the workings of the balance of nature.* (Oxford Scientific Films)